Facilitator's Guide

More
Inclusion Strategies
That Work!

Facilitator's Guide

More Inclusion Strategies That Work!

Aligning Student Strengths With Standards

Toby J. Karten

CORWIN PRESS
A SAGE Company
Thousand Oaks, CA 91320

For information:

Corwin Press
A SAGE Company
2455 Teller Road
Thousand Oaks, California 91320
www.corwinpress.com

SAGE Ltd.
1 Oliver's Yard
55 City Road
London EC1Y 1SP
United Kingdom

SAGE India Pvt. Ltd.
B 1/I 1 Mohan Cooperative
    Industrial Area
Mathura Road, New Delhi 110 044
India

SAGE Asia-Pacific Pte. Ltd.
33 Pekin Street #02-01
Far East Square
Singapore 048763

Printed in the United States of America

ISBN: 978-1-4129-6484-5

This book is printed on acid-free paper.

08   09   10   11   12   10   9   8   7   6   5   4   3   2   1

Acquisitions Editor:	David Chao
Editorial Assistant:	Mary Dang
Production Editor:	Melanie Birdsall
Copy Editor:	Teresa Herlinger
Typesetter:	C&M Digitals (P) Ltd.
Proofreader:	Cheryl Rivard
Cover Designer:	Monique Hahn

Contents

About the Author

Toby J. Karten is an adjunct professor at the College of New Jersey, Gratz College in Pennsylvania, and Washington College in Maryland. Along with being a mentor and resource center teacher in New Jersey, Karten has designed a graduate course titled "Skills and Strategies for Inclusion and disABILITY Awareness" and has trained other instructors to teach her course. Karten has presented at local, state, national, and international staff development workshops and conferences. She has been recognized by both the Council for Exceptional Children and the New Jersey Department of Education as an exemplary educator, receiving two "Teacher of the Year" awards. Karten has authored several books for Corwin Press about inclusion practices, including *Inclusion Strategies That Work!* and *More Inclusion Strategies That Work!* as well as a series of activity books. An experienced educator who has worked in the field of special education since 1976, Karten believes that once we place the adjective *special* in front of the noun *education*, every classroom student is a winner, receiving the best instructional strategies by a highly trained and prepared staff. She has an undergraduate degree in special education from Brooklyn College, a master of science degree in special education from the College of Staten Island, and a supervisory degree from Georgian Court University.

Introduction

How to Use the Guide

This facilitator's guide is a companion to *More Inclusion Strategies That Work! Aligning Student Strengths With Standards.* It is designed to accompany the study of the book and provide assistance to group facilitators, such as school leaders, professional development coordinators, peer coaches, team leaders, mentors, and professors. Along with a summary of each chapter in the book, Toby J. Karten has provided chapter discussion questions, activities, journal writing prompts, suggestions for practical application, and resources for extending learning. When using the guide during independent study, focus on the summaries, practical applications, and discussion questions.

For small study groups, the facilitator should guide the group through the chapter work.

For small- or large-group workshops, the facilitator should create an agenda by selecting activities and discussion starters from the chapter reviews that meet the group's goals, and guide the group through the learning process. Sample half-day, one-day, and two-day agendas are also offered. Facilitators can follow these or create their own as well.

Additional Resources for Facilitators

Corwin Press also offers a free 16-page resource titled *Tips for Facilitators,* which includes practical strategies and tips for guiding a successful meeting. The information in this section describes different professional development opportunities, the principles of effective professional development, some characteristics of an effective facilitator, the responsibilities of the facilitator, and practical tips and strategies to make the meeting more successful. *Tips for*

Facilitators is available for free download at the Corwin Press Web site (www.corwinpress.com, under "Resources").

We recommend that facilitators download a copy of *Tips for Facilitators* and review the characteristics and responsibilities of facilitators and professional development strategies for different types of work groups and settings.

Preface

This facilitator's guide offers insights and strategies about how educators can capitalize on and maximize the strengths of students of all abilities in inclusive classrooms. The curriculum standards are outlined with a matching list of accommodations and modifications offered for students with different abilities. Educators can implement these inclusion strategies to instruct students with differing cognitive, sensory, physical, behavioral, emotional, and social levels. When used in a collegial atmosphere of learning, it is hoped that teachers will be empowered by the guide's activities to creatively translate the best inclusive practices into their own classrooms on a daily basis.

The format and carefully chosen activities are explicitly designed to stimulate more discussion and thoughts about pragmatic inclusive practices with reflective questions, journal entries, practical applications, and further resources. Baseline, advancing, and more challenging assignments and objectives are demonstrated through diverse curriculum lessons. The guide is meant to assist educators in their efforts to have students not only meet the standards but surpass them as well. The students entrusted to the care of school systems deserve only the best inclusive efforts we as educators can offer to help them expand their life potentials.

Inclusive classroom successes will not end within the pages of *More Inclusion Strategies That Work! Aligning Strengths With Standards,* but will face the true test of inclusion when students are offered dynamic classroom lessons that implement the ideas, strategies, and practices. This guide's purpose is to motivate educators to continue in that inclusive direction. If this guide stimulates further thought and helps teachers view inclusion not only as a feasible program but as a viable one, then as the author, I have achieved my goal of sharing the *inclusive wealth!*

Chapter-by-Chapter Study Guide

Facilitator's Guide to
More Inclusion Strategies That Work!
Aligning Student Strengths With Standards
by Toby J. Karten

Part I. Fundamentals of Honoring Potentials and Strengths of Students and Teachers

Chapter 1. Concentrating on Students' Strengths and Curriculum Standards

Summary With Practical Applications

Students in inclusive classrooms are often assigned tasks that do not tap into their strengths and coursework that ignores their interests or abilities. Metacognition and self-advocacy are essential inclusive elements for teachers and students. Being cognizant of individual students' interests and strengths allows students to shine, both emotionally and academically. Rather than just answering specific questions related to the facts presented in Chapter 1, educators are given activities that allow them to creatively apply the knowledge through synthesis and evaluation to expand and stretch their own classroom repertoires. Students in inclusive classrooms need the opportunity to display their learning in a variety of ways as well, to develop better critical thinking skills across the curriculum. Although an inclusion template does not exist, the implementation of sound basic educational principles ensures that classrooms are designed to not only welcome but also enhance the inclusion of students with and without disabilities to experience successful outcomes. Research supports the ongoing merits of inclusion, but the teachers are the ones who ultimately transfer this research into effective classroom practices with accommodations designed to help but not enable their students.

Discussion Questions

1. Can disabilities have positive characteristics?
2. What can teachers do to maximize the strengths of students with disabilities, yet not sacrifice the learning of other students?
3. Do accommodations or modifications jade the resulting learning outcomes?
4. How can curriculum standards be applied to classroom lessons, if all students do not have the same entering prior knowledge?

Activities

a. Strategically Starting With Strengths

Time: 30 minutes
Materials: Index cards

Facilitator gives each participant an index card to anonymously create an individualized list of his or her top five strengths, for example, perceptive, mechanical, philosophical, analytical, compassionate, and organized. The facilitator then collects the index cards, shuffles them, and distributes one to each person in the group. The next step is to ask each participant to decide what profession he or she thinks the person on the card would best be suited for, and a profession that would probably be the worst choice for that person. If a person has his or her own card, then advise that person to be self-reflective and not share that information with others until the end of the activity. Collectively, the class shares the accommodation or modification choices. The group draws conclusions about how sometimes it's difficult to expect people and students to conform to assigned job responsibilities or classroom standards.

b. Stepping Into the Classroom: Best Versus Worst Scenarios

Time: 30–40 minutes
Materials: *More Inclusion Strategies That Work! Aligning Student Strengths With Standards* (pages 6–25)

Ask participants to TTYP (Talk to Your Peer/Partner). Together, each pair selects positive characteristics of two disabilities listed on pages 6–25 and writes classroom dialogue that tells the academic, behavioral, and physical reactions of students during a given lesson on _____. Allow participants to fill in the blanks to select their own subject, based upon personal experiences, population, age group, and applicability. If the group is a larger one, then participants can TTTQ (Talk to Their Quartet or Quintet) and role-play a classroom scenario/dialogue for students, teachers, or coteachers to capitalize on students' strengths in inclusive classrooms.

c. Inclusion PAYS

Time: 30–40 minutes
Materials: *More Inclusion Strategies That Work! Aligning Student Strengths With Standards* (page 39 and research quotes as outlined on pages 4–25), journals

Educators follow instructions delineated on page 39 and choose two quotes about students with differences and/or the standards from Chapter 1. If participants prefer to have more room to write their responses, they can divide lined paper into three columns, heading the first with a letter *P* to paraphrase the quotes; the second column with the letter *A* to analyze the quotes, saying whether they agree or disagree; and the third column with the letter *Y*, standing for you, and how the quotes relate to their teaching practices. The facilitator can also share other education and journal articles to involve the group in additional district-specific curriculum research.

Self-Reflection and Journal Writing Prompts

d. Inclusion Poem

Do you think that sometimes classroom activities are unsuited for students with disabilities? Why does a deficit paradigm limit the potentials of students with disabilities? Read the *Inclusion Poem* in the preface (page ix) and tell if you think it has applicable classroom merits. Could you add your own stanza to the poem?

Resources for Extending Your Learning

The following books, organizations, and online sites are recommended for extending your learning in the areas of strengths, standards, and disabilities.

Council for Exceptional Children. (2003). *What every special educator must know: Ethics, standards, and guidelines for special educators.* Arlington, VA: Author.

Gregory, G., & Chapman, C. (2002). *Differentiated instructional strategies: One size doesn't fit all.* Thousand Oaks, CA: Corwin Press.

Klass, P., & Costello, E. (2003). *Quirky kids.* New York: Ballantine Books.

National Dissemination Center for Children with Disabilities. http://www.nichcy.org.

Mid-continent Research for Education and Learning. www.mcrel .org/standards-benchmarks.

Pierangelo, R., & Giuliani, G. (2007). *EDM: The educator's diagnostic manual of disabilities and disorders.* San Francisco: Jossey-Bass.

Encourage educators to refer to their own state standards and resources as listed in *More Inclusion Strategies That Work! Aligning Student Strengths With Standards* on pages 5–6. Pages 27–32 also offer specific information about disabilities, curriculum, and inclusion.

Chapter 2. Understanding Assessments and Curriculum Standards

Summary With Practical Applications

If students in inclusive classrooms are to be successful, then both instruction and assessments must be sensitive to individuals by honoring students' differing abilities. Special education is not a separate way of teaching, but a philosophy that advocates solid educational practices to help all learners improve individual skills to maximize their assets. Achievements in both academic and functional/life skills happen when educators teach students, not just subjects. Classrooms that are proactively designed allow for student differences, while honoring students' strengths, interests, and preferred modalities, with the delivery of applicable instructional strategies and assessments. Auditory learners listen better to instruction and are more attentive to oral questions, while visual learners prefer ways to *show what they know* through images. Allowing students to have assessment options, such as the ones listed on page 52, honors individual strengths and interests, inviting students to experience the joys and satisfaction of learning, beyond the skill-and-drill approach.

Discussion Questions

1. How can assessments gauge teachers' plans? Why is documentation essential?
2. Does *fair* mean *equal* in terms of assignments and assessments?
3. Is there a way to acknowledge students' efforts and progress, rather than focusing solely upon their achievements?

Activities

a. Band-Aid Activity

Time: 10–15 minutes
Materials: Four Band-Aids

Randomly deliver the following dialogue to four participants and then hand each of the four people a Band-Aid.

- Dialogue to the first person: "I heard that your pet hermit frog was not feeling well. Here's a Band-Aid."
- Dialogue to the second person: "Sorry to hear that you are sad today. Here's a Band-Aid."
- Dialogue to the third person: "Sorry to hear that you did not pass your chemistry test. Here's a Band-Aid."
- Dialogue to the fourth person: "Here's a Band-Aid for your cut finger."

Practical applications: The major point is that not everyone needed the Band-Aid, and such an intervention was appropriate for only one person. The same principle can be applied to classroom ssignments and assessments. Equality is not always the classroom reality!

b. Ways to Assess the French and Indian War

Time: 60–75 minutes
Materials: *More Inclusion Strategies That Work! Aligning Student Strengths With Standards* (pages 50–54)

The roles of Narrator, French, George Washington, Ben Franklin, Iroquois, British, Pontiac, Colonists, and Sons of Liberty are acted out by *would-be/want-to-be educational thespians*. After the play, everyone collectively reviews and discusses the Sample Assessment that lists four different assignments based upon the play's content. Then invite participants to cooperatively or individually think of an *instructional twist* to a curriculum topic or concept and decide on three different ways they would assess their students' knowledge, as described on page 54 in the three-columned chart. Share finished products as time permits.

c. Inclusion Rubric: Appropriate Instructional Strategies and Assessments

Time: 15–20 minutes
Materials: Handout 1

The group is instructed to fill in the table on Handout 1 by placing the letters of each descriptor under the correct column headings of *excellent, good, fair,* and *noninclusive* practices. After allowing participants a chance to independently fill in the chart, the facilitator invites responses for a collective discussion.

Self-Reflection and Journal Writing Prompts

d. The ABCD Quarterly Checklist of Functional Objectives

The ABCD Quarterly Checklist of Functional Objectives on page 53 has nonacademic areas evaluated at quarterly periods. How do these *nonacademic indicators* affect academics? Should teachers be held accountable for students' noncompliance or regression in either academic or nonacademic domains?

Resources for Extending Your Learning

Educational Psychology Topics, Perspectives on Teaching. http:// mhhe.com/socscience/education/edpsych/edpsytop.html.

Harcourt Assessment: Learnia with answer analysis at http://harcourt assessment.com.

Nolet, V., & McLaughlin, M. (2005). *Accessing the general curriculum: Including students with disabilities in standards-based reform.* Thousand Oaks, CA: Corwin Press.

Nunley, K. (2006). *Differentiating the high school classroom: Solution strategies for 18 common obstacles.* Thousand Oaks, CA: Corwin Press.

Chapter 3. How Students Learn: Brain Basics

Summary With Practical Applications

Emotions can positively or negatively influence learning outcomes. As research indicates, classrooms that value brain-based learning are more likely to attain ongoing student achievements. Education is about *planting seeds,* with *roots* for students to develop a love of learning, which *stems* from nurturing inclusive environments. Students with emotional issues need more empowerment and motivation that acknowledge and value the cognitive and affective connections.

Discussion Questions

1. Explain why you agree or disagree with Zull's statement on page 56 that learning should feel good, and the student should become aware of those feelings.
2. How can prior experiences impact a student's education?
3. Are people intelligent in *multiple ways*?

Activities

● *a. Smart Chart*

Time: 15–20 minutes
Materials: *More Inclusion Strategies That Work! Aligning Student Strengths With Standards* (pages 59–60), Handout 2

After pages 59–60 on multiple intelligences are reviewed, the facilitator guides participants to fill in Handout 2 to match letter descriptors of present and future people with their preferred or stronger intelligences. Share responses depending on available time.

● **b. Pledge With an Edge**

Time: 5–10 minutes
Materials: *More Inclusion Strategies That Work! Aligning Student Strengths With Standards* (page 64, Student Pledge)

Facilitator reads the beginning part of each line while participants chorally fill in the end rhyming words. The major focus is to concentrate on students' motivations to be both physically and emotionally an integral stakeholder in classroom lessons. The pledge on page 65 is geared for younger learners or those learners who require differently leveled vocabulary. Encourage educators to ask their own students to recite these pledges or cooperatively create their own pledge and learning symbol as noted on pages 63–65.

● **c. Looking Back to Move Ahead**

Time: 20–30 minutes
Materials: Handout 3 with intrapersonal connections

Facilitator asks participants to think back to a prior lesson, topic, or instruction they experienced as a student or learner and use the Venn diagram to compare and contrast their understandings, from then to now. Facilitator asks the group to reflect on how their prior knowledge or lack of prior knowledge influenced their learning strides, or if repeated instruction and review were required for mastery. Topics can include Pilates, watercolor instruction, and assembling furniture, or educational subjects such as understanding calculus or instructing students with autism. As an option, a participant can instead fill in the Venn diagram for a student's learning progress, keeping names confidential.

Self-Reflection and Journal Writing Prompts

● **d. Multiple Intelligences**

Review the chart on page 59 on Multiple Intelligences and choose your favorite and least preferred intelligence. Do you often shy away from tapping into your least preferred intelligence while designing your own classroom lessons? How can you as an educator help students to develop skills to circumvent their weaker intelligences?

Resources for Extending Your Learning

Fogarty, R., & Stoehr, J. (2007). *Integrating curricula with multiple intelligences.* Thousand Oaks, CA: Corwin Press.

Garner, B. (2007). *Getting to got it: Helping struggling students learn how to learn.* Alexandria, VA: Association for Supervision and Curriculum Development.

Sousa, D. (2005). *How the brain learns to read.* Thousand Oaks, CA: Corwin Press.

Sylwester, R. (2005). *How to explain a brain.* Thousand Oaks, CA: Corwin Press.

Willis, J. (2007). *Brain-friendly strategies for the inclusion classroom.* Alexandria, VA: Association for Supervision and Curriculum Development.

Chapter 4. How Teachers Teach: Good Practices for All

Summary With Practical Applications

Inclusive instructional practices benefit all learners when they offer students proactive, metacognitive strategies that honor students' individual levels and abilities. Frequent formal and informal monitoring helps a teacher determine if students understand the concepts and, at the same time, gauges instruction. Inclusive strategies need not be complex ones, but ones that include a variety of practices for alternate delivery of content, sometimes with more repetition, and at other times, more acceleration. Some students respond best to a semiabstract level, while others require multisensory, kinesthetic/ concrete elements, or even mnemonic devices. In addition, when staff and home environments collaborate to prepare for student successes, the results are worthwhile ones. Effective inclusion practices create life-long learners who no longer consider themselves as separate or apart from the general education population, but an integral part of the classroom, and then society as a whole.

Discussion Questions

1. How can educators divide themselves and students in manageable inclusive classrooms?
2. Is it feasible to vary the complexity and pace of lessons, yet still expect students to achieve desired learning objectives?
3. How can ongoing communication, collaboration, documentation, and reflection change and guide lessons?

Activities

● *a. Good Practices*

Time: 20–30 minutes
Materials: *More Inclusion Strategies That Work! Aligning Student Strengths With Standards* (pages 70–71)

Ask participants to compare and contrast Valuable and Applicable Things to Do in All Classrooms on a Daily Basis on page 71

(Figure 4.2), with Inclusion Strategies That Work! on page 70 (Figure 4.1 with the boxed pictures), and tell which they prefer. Both pages have the same information, with more written details in Figure 4.2, while visuals accompany the terse text in Figure 4.1. Invite the participants to add ideas or drawings to the list of 18 points. Participants must understand that even if educators may prefer one presentation over the other, the preferences of some of their students will vary and not match their choices. Instruction needs to be cognizant of the teacher–student spectrum.

b. Strategies People Search

Time: 40–50 minutes
Materials: 18 index cards with numbers 1–18 consecutively printed on each, to match the delineated 18 strategies (see *More Inclusion Strategies That Work! Aligning Student Strengths With Standards,* page 71, Figure 4.2), Handout 4

The numbered index cards are divided among the participants. If a group of nine people is in the workshop, then each person is given two cards, while a group of 36–40 people would have each group of two or three people sharing a numbered card. The next step is for each person or group to collaboratively think of a way that their strategies can be applied and translated into classroom scenarios or lessons. For example, if someone held a card with number 17, then that person or group of people would think of a way to increase students' self-awareness of levels and progress, such as having a student graph his or her weekly spelling test grades. Each person then writes his or her idea by the appropriately numbered line on Handout 4. After each group decides upon their classroom connection, ideas are shared with other groups until each of the lines by the 18 numbers is filled in with different classroom applications. The facilitator circulates about while the participants are creating and sharing their strategies.

c. Note-Taking Acronym: TEST the GAME CORD

Time: 20–30 minutes
Materials: Overhead 1

The purpose of this activity is to outline major inclusive factors for educators in a way that they will remember and apply the knowledge for best classroom practice and continual implementation. The facilitator fills in each representative word on Overhead 1 as participants take notes and write the associative words next to the corresponding letters. As the words are given, a brief lecturette and class discussion with a recommended facilitator's script is given to delineate the points below.

T = Teachers	**G** = Gather	**C** = Communication/
E = Environments	**A** = Apply	Collaboration
S = Students	**M** = Manipulate	**O** = Organization
T = Topics	**E** = Evaluate	**R** = Reflection
		D = Documentation

The first acronymic word, TEST, refers to the fact that inclusion will vary depending on the teachers, environments, students, and topics. Knowledge, preparation, experience, motivation, support, resources, and inclusion location vary across the board.

This leads to the second word, GAME, which means that given the same topic, some students may appropriately be required to just gather the facts or knowledge, while other students may apply, manipulate, or evaluate learning principles. This too may vary depending on the students' prior knowledge and mastery of each topic as the curriculum spirals. Students with differing cognitive levels or behavioral needs may require parallel assignments or additional guided supervision by adults and peers, while those with more advanced levels need to have their strengths honored with appropriate instruction and activities to extend their learning. The most important point is that all students are learning, but at different paces and degrees of complexity.

Now comes the CORD, which continually connects all inclusive players to the learning. *C* for collaboration means that teachers communicate with families, students, administration, coteachers, and all staff and faculty to ensure that the learning is valued and supported across school and home settings. Next comes the *O* for organizational plans and the *R* referring to reflective lessons for teachers and students that outline learning objectives. *D* for documentation includes realistic and ongoing dated assessments and anecdotal records of achievements and efforts. Sometimes the staff at school may not be privy to students' thoughts and different behavior displayed at home or even other classes. In conclusion, when teachers *TEST the GAME CORD,* many more connections are possible!

d. Connecting the GAME CORD

Time: 30–40 minutes
Materials: *More Inclusion Strategies That Work! Aligning Student Strengths With Standards* (page 73, Figure 4.3; page 79)

The facilitator asks teachers to pair up into teams based upon their grade levels, assignments, populations taught, or randomly if that division is more appropriate. Teachers select a skill and objective from page 79, letters A to LL, and compose a class of students with different needs from numbers 1 to 23. The two lists are then collated with participants differentiating assignments to increase each student's baseline knowledge while honoring the advancing levels of other students present. The acronym GAME is applied to allow some students to Gather facts, while others Apply, Manipulate, or Evaluate the selected learning concepts, skills, and objectives. The facilitator guides the pairs to think about the division of assignments in an inclusive classroom by reviewing page 73 in reference to instructional styles, curriculum concerns, modifications, accommodations, testing, grading, and classroom rules. When the class gathers together as a whole, pairs exchange inclusion ideas, strategies, and concerns.

Self-Reflection and Journal Writing Prompts

Ask participants to identify visuals that help them perform everyday tasks and to note possible consequences if the visuals were not present. How would the complexity or performance of the task be affected? Do you agree with the statement, *A picture is worth a thousand words*?

Why do some learners lose attention during classroom lectures? Is it possible to teach the same learning concepts to help students meet and achieve academic standards without requiring students to sit in traditional classrooms with an *all heads facing forward, take notes* method?

Have you ever been in a learning situation where you felt overwhelmed, yet kept quiet for fear of being viewed as incompetent or not as sharp as the others? What or who helped you to overcome or circumvent these difficulties? If you could go back to a given situation, would you communicate your needs differently?

Resources for Extending Your Learning

Review and discuss *More Inclusion Strategies That Work! Aligning Student Strengths With Standards*, pages 42–47 in sections labeled Grading Issues, Studying and Teaching for More Than the Test, Other Assessment Options, *Testy* Language, Interpreting Data, and Empowering Students by Demystifying the Grading System, along with pages 25–26, Enabling Versus Challenging Your Students, pages 69–77, Collaboration, Coteaching, and Preparation, and the forms for Classroom Documentations and Communications on pages 295–297.

Part II. Standards-Based Inclusion Strategies That Work

Chapter 5. Standards-Based Reading Objectives

Summary With Practical Applications

Some students' brains are not wired to automatically learn how to read without receiving explicit direct skill instruction. Learning to read and succeed with the printed word is an evolutionary process that requires students to be able to not only decode and encode unfamiliar words but also to comprehend a variety of genres and vocabulary in fiction and nonfiction texts, news-papers, magazines, prose, and journals. This chapter explores syllabication, structural analysis, and critical thinking skills to help learners improve their fluency, word identification, and reading comprehension. Some students need a combination of strategies, such as auditory, visual, and kinesthetic ones, to become better readers. All students need to make sense of the reading process by unlocking the code to find rules and patterns with syllables, prefixes, and vocabulary across the curriculum. In addition, teaching students how to look for reading clues with charts, captions, or italicized and bolded words helps them to determine the main idea without focusing on extraneous details that, although they may prove interesting, distract from understanding what the author or writer is trying to delineate. The most important practical application is that students need to know that reading connects to every subject, including life!

Discussion Questions

1. How can teachers help students who *hate to read*?
2. Have you encountered students with lower reading levels who mask their misunderstandings under the guise of misbehavior, rather than admitting that they need extra help?
3. Should there be a core vocabulary list that all students across each grade master?
4. How can teachers in inclusive classrooms honor the integrity of an older student, without singling him or her out as a slower learner or reader?
5. What strategies can teachers share with families to help their children improve reading skills, from the early grades onward?

Activities

a. Unsequenced Syllables and Prefixes

Time: 10–15 minutes
Materials: *More Inclusion Strategies That Work! Aligning Student Strengths With Standards* (page 92, Figure 5.3a; page 96, Figure 5.5; pages 97–99, Figure 5.6)

Ask participants to choose a curriculum topic and think of content-related words with two, three, and four syllables. As depicted in Figure 5.3, the next step is to divide the words into their syllables and then scramble them to better concentrate on the individual syllables, rather than the entire words. Afterward, try to decide which column in Figure 5.5 each syllable belongs to, for example, closed, open, consonant—le, vowel—e, vowel digraphs, r-controlled, or vowel diphthongs. Next, try to chart content words with prefixes.

b. SOARing Into Reading

Time: 20–30 minutes
Materials: *More Inclusion Strategies That Work! Aligning Student Strengths With Standards* (page 101, Figure 5.8), assorted magazines, journals, textbooks, and/or curriculum-related nonfiction books, lined paper

The facilitator demonstrates the SOAR technique as shown on page 101 using a nonfiction reading selection of about five to eight pages. The facilitator scans the pages and points out the illustrations and charts, bold letters, headings, subheadings, captions, and highlighted words. Then the facilitator takes a piece of paper and folds it into three columns, heading the first one with the letter M, then D, and then Y. As a class, based upon the facts delineated from the scanning, the main idea is extracted and outlined under the column that is labeled *M* for the main idea. Then the class collectively analyzes and reviews the pages again before an actual reading, to achieve a better understanding of the topic. The facilitator reminds the class that the second column, *D,* which stands for the details, is filled in only after pages are read. The *Y* column is filled in last, when a personal connection is made. After the facilitator models the SOARing technique, each person is asked to choose his or her own journal, magazine, or text, including this text, to select an article or a few pages to *SOAR* and to fill in his or her own M/D/Y chart.

Self-Reflection and Journal Writing Prompts

Have you ever preferred to listen to a book on tape rather than read a hard copy? Have you read a book and then been disappointed when you saw the movie? Were the characters as you envisioned them in the book? Did you ever need to read directions more than once to fully understand how to assemble something or perhaps follow a recipe?

Resources for Extending Your Learning

Allen, J. (2007). *Inside words: Tools for teaching academic vocabulary, Grades 4–12*. Portland, ME: Stenhouse.

Content Standards for the English Language Arts. http://www.ncte.org/. Developed by the National Council of Teachers of English (NCTE) and the International Reading Association (IRA).

Downing, J. (2005). *Teaching literacy to students with significant disabilities*. Thousand Oaks, CA: Corwin Press.

Karten, T. (2007). *Inclusion activities that work! Grades K–2, 3–5, 6–8*. Thousand Oaks, CA: Corwin Press.

Karten, T. (2007). *Inclusion strategies that work! Research-based methods for the classroom*. Thousand Oaks, CA: Corwin Press. Resource has specific stations and rubrics for students to demonstrate their understandings of fiction and nonfiction readings, for example, research, performance, word, picture, and teacher station.

Orton-Gillingham Institute for Multi-sensory Education. http://www.orton-gillingham.com/orton-gillingham4.asp.

Chapter 6. Standards–Based Writing, Listening, and Speaking Objectives

Summary With Practical Applications

Just like its close cousin, reading, writing has many genres such as autobiography, fiction, nonfiction, essays, letters, cartoons, editorials, poetry, newspaper articles, and more. Writing also has many specific purposes, such as informing, persuading, reflecting, and communicating to different audiences. When students demonstrate their knowledge through written assessments across curriculum topics, they have achieved a greater mastery of the concepts and details. Many students need guided writing lessons with personalized connections, tools, and models to help them be less fearful of the whole writing process. Students with organizational difficulties or dysgraphia can be taught to be productive writers with step-by-step modeling, more technology, and peer or teacher guidance. Ultimately, learning how to listen and speak appropriately is a vital communicative skill that will enhance every child's school experiences, future career decisions, and daily activities. Writing is a form of communication that students must perceive of as a fun activity, not a chore!

Discussion Questions

1. Why do many students who are frequent *doodlers* dislike conventional writing?
2. Do you think that students who keep journals in different subject areas are more reflective learners? Have you ever kept a journal or dated log?

3. How has e-mailing and text messaging influenced the conventions of writing, for example, capitalization, punctuation, spelling, sentence structure, and vocabulary?
4. How can teachers help students with attention and organizational issues learn to develop better note-taking skills?

Activities

a. Expanding Upon Inclusion: ED'S CAR

Time: 20–30 minutes
Materials: Lined paper and *More Inclusion Strategies That Work! Aligning Student Strengths With Standards* (page 117, Figure 6.8, *ABC*ing Your Thoughts with ED'S CAR graphic and acronym; page 111, Figure 6.4, Stop and Think Sheet; page 114, Words to Connect Thoughts; page 112, Figure 6.5, ED'S CAR rules modeled)

The facilitator asks the group to write words next to each letter from A–Z on page 117 about positive ways to approach inclusion. If participants wish to save the page for classroom duplication and student usage and do not want to write in the book, then they can just vertically list the alphabet from A–Z in the left margin of lined paper and free associate inclusive words. The next step is for participants to write the word *inclusion* in the center and fill in the planning web on page 111 with answers to *wh* questions such as

- Who is involved in the inclusion process?
- When can effective inclusion be accomplished?
- Why is inclusion a way of life?
- Where is the least restrictive environment?
- What are appropriate inclusion strategies classroom teachers can implement?
- How can lessons be written to accommodate different learner needs?

Then the facilitator directs each person to organize his or her thoughts by placing the numbers 1, 2, and 3 by some of the A–Z words and answers to the web questions, which sequentially refer to the beginning, middle, and conclusion of a three-paragraph essay on inclusion. Next, each person in the group reviews the two planners, *ABCing Your Thoughts* and the *Stop and Think* web, to write an expository piece on positive approaches to inclusion. Remind participants to skip lines as they write, leaving room for revisions. After an initial writing draft of the three paragraphs, the facilitator invites the group to review the ED'S CAR acronym on page 117 and Figure 6.5 on page 112, which delineates expanding, deleting, substituting, and combining and rearranging words and thoughts expressed in sentences. Also, instruct the group to review the list of transitional words on page 114 and add appropriate ones as needed. Remind the group to frequently reread and edit their own work until they are satisfied with the mechanics, word choices, sentence structure, and thoughts conveyed. Final copies can then be orally shared, typed, and even self-published into a bound book for the group titled *Positive Inclusive Approaches*. If more time is needed, participants can finish this at their own pace as a culminating project. Encourage educators to turnkey these strategies with their students.

Self-Reflection and Journal Writing Prompts

Do you plan to write a book one day? If you were to do so, describe your intended audience. How many times have you called someone on the telephone or waited for a face-to-face meeting, rather than putting your thoughts down in writing? How did the writing planners influence your piece on inclusion?

Resources for Extending Your Learning

Gess, D. (2006). *Teaching writing: Strategies for improving literacy across the curriculum.* Suffern, NY: The Write Track. Available at http://www.thewritetrack.com.

Inspiration/Kidspiration Software. http://www.inspiration.com. Strengthens critical thinking, comprehension, and writing across the curriculum with increased graphic organizers, outlines, and more visuals.

Jacobs, H. (2006). *Active literacy across the curriculum: Strategies for reading, writing, speaking, and listening.* Larchmont, NY: Eye on Education.

Mayer-Johnson. http://www.mayer-johnson.com. Provides communication tools, for example, boardmakers, interactive producats, AAC products.

Slater Software. http://www.slatersoftware.com. Picture-assisted literacy.

Chapter 7. Standards-Based Math Objectives

Summary With Practical Applications

Just like words are a part of our world, numbers are too! Mathematics is about understanding shapes, patterns, values, estimation, relationships, and logical ways to solve everyday problems. Some students with dyscalculia do not process information the same way as other learners. Their difficulties with one-to-one correspondence, sequencing, memory, organization, measurements, and spatial relationships may interfere with understandings. Many of these students become almost *math phobic*, hating numbers and never connecting the skills to life. A classroom store, mock restaurant, and math centers and stations are practical ways to allow students to cooperatively manipulate numbers with interpersonal connections that strengthen computations and logical reasoning, without solely using boring textbook examples. In addition, interdisciplinary connections in reading, science, social studies, and more send out a strong message that math does not exist in a vacuum, but is very well connected to our lives. Journals for older students or picture math for younger and more concrete learners increase understandings. Success breeds success, and as with other disciplines, students need multiple opportunities to demonstrate, improve, and apply their proficiencies in inclusive mathematics lessons that model the skills and guide them.

Discussion Questions

1. Have you ever been shopping in a store when the power went off and the cashier could not make change?
2. How can calculators both enhance and sometimes thwart mathematical growth?
3. Describe how a student's attitude influences his or her mathematical performance.

Activities

a. Math for Life!

Time: 20 minutes
Materials: *More Inclusion Strategies That Work! Aligning Student Strengths With Standards* (page 129, Figure 7.2; page 133, Figure 7.7; page 135, Figure 7.9; page 138, Figure 7.12; page 139, Figure 7.13)

The facilitator divides the group into quadrants, asking each of the groups to connect math topics from the above figures with life examples. Afterward, the quadrants form a whole again and share their mathematical applications.

b. Problem Solving: Inclusive Strategies

Time: 30 minutes
Materials: *More Inclusion Strategies That Work! Aligning Student Strengths With Standards* (page 134, Figure 7.8), Handout 5

Participants estimate, guess and check, draw a picture, make a list, dissect problems, create a chart or table, look for a pattern, work backward, act out problems, use logical reasoning, solve a simpler problem, or set up an equation to cooperatively solve the *inclusion word problems* on Handout 5.

● *c. Reading the Math*

Time: 15 minutes
Materials: Handout 6

The group solves mathematical computations and equations on Handout 6 to discover the goal of special education, or in fact the goal of all education. The group matches its answers with the alphabetical code. The blank lines are intended for those participants who finish before others to create their own mathematical problems.

Self-Reflection and Journal Writing Prompts

How would you rank the subject of mathematics on a scale of 1–10, with the rating of 10 if it's your favorite subject, and a 1 if mathematics is your least favorite subject? Estimate the number of times that you use math in your daily activities.

Resources for Extending Your Learning

Abeel, S. (2003). *My thirteenth winter.* New York: Scholastic News. (A memoir about dyscalculia)
Content Standards for Mathematics. http://standards.nctm.org. Developed by the National Council of Teachers of Mathematics (NCTM).
Factor Frenzy. http://www.educationallearninggames.com/factor-frenzy.asp.
Hirsch, C. (Ed.). (2007). *Perspectives on design and development of school mathematics curricula.* National Council of Teachers of Mathematics. Available at http://www.nctm.org/publications.
Silva, J. (2004). *Teaching inclusive mathematics for special learners, K–6.* Thousand Oaks, CA: Corwin Press.
Sudoku. http://www.soduko.org/sudoku-play-online.php.
Tang, G. (2005). *Math for all seasons.* New York: Scholastic Paperbacks.
Web sites: www.aplusmath.com, www.funbrain.com.

Chapter 8. Standards-Based Science and Technology Objectives

Summary With Practical Applications

Inquiry is an integral ingredient for not only the subject of science but for learners in all disciplines. Logical thinking is required to analyze outcomes and the effects of variables in both constructed experiments and natural life occurrences. Technology is a field of science and engineering that involves students using tools to not only increase their knowledge but also to organize, manipulate, and interpret their findings in logical ways. Students with lower reading abilities should not be thwarted from demonstrating their knowledge in other subject areas, such as science. Some students may love science but be unable to read the text or follow a set of written directions. Teachers need to be sensitive to this by allowing students to gain knowledge in creative ways, for example, more content-related visuals for each unit and preteaching vocabulary. Accommodations for students with different emotional, physical, sensory, and learning needs do not necessarily need to be intricate ones, for example, larger-size font on worksheets, amplification systems, more frequent breaks, concrete experiments, modeling, talking Web sites, or word prediction programs. After accommodations are given, proactive educators can guide students to develop better critical thinking skills in the subject of science and beyond.

Discussion Questions

1. Why do you think students need to *see the science*?
2. How can teachers use the classroom and school environments as *learning laboratories*?
3. Describe circumstances that involve students of all ages as scientists and researchers.

Activities

a. Science Levels and Accommodations for All Students

Time: 30 minutes
Materials: *More Inclusion Strategies That Work! Aligning Student Strengths With Standards* (pages 143–168), Handout 7

Cooperative groups jigsaw the chart on Handout 7, dependent upon interests, to fill in one of the rows/concepts. Groups review appropriate science and technology topic sections on pages 143–168 to gain insights about specific standards, strategies, and accommodations. Each group then demonstrates a science lesson, with everyone seeing how to differentiate objectives for learners in inclusive science classrooms.

Self-Reflection and Journal Writing Prompts

Do you think that some students have greater technological acumen than their teachers?

Can schools keep pace with the increasing scientific knowledge and ever-changing technology? Would you like more professional development opportunities in the fields of science and technology? How can you help students to hone their skills of observation and attention to detail while delivering the science curriculum?

Resources for Extending Your Learning

Assistive Technology News. http://www.atechnews.com.

CAST: Center for Applied Special Technology. http://www.cast.org.

Gregory, G., & Hammerman, E. (2007). *Differentiated instructional strategies for science, Grades K–8.* Thousand Oaks, CA: Corwin Press.

Llewellyn, D. (2005). *Teaching high school science through inquiry.* Thousand Oaks, CA: Corwin Press.

NSTA Journals: National Science Teacher's Association. http://www.nsta .org/publications/journals.aspx (*Science Scope; The Science Teacher*).

Chapter 9. Standards-Based Social Studies Objectives

Summary With Practical Applications

Understanding about the workings of governments, world history, cultural awareness, current events, economics, and geography will not be achieved unless teachers find innovative ways to relate these topics to students. As with other subjects, it is vital to assess prior knowledge in terms of social studies vocabulary and concepts to prevent misconceptions from arising. Effective inclusive classrooms establish baseline knowledge standards, combined with advancing levels and objectives for those students who may need more challenging assignments. Very often difficulties with time concepts, sequencing, organization, attention to detail, decoding, encoding, and comprehension thwart students' social studies successes. Videos, visuals, field trips, and photographs allow primary and secondary sources to mesh and build blocks for solid social studies foundations. Social studies needs to come alive and enter students' lives, helping them to understand not just the facts and dates, but what implications the concepts and vocabulary had then, have now, and will have in future generations!

Discussion Questions

1. Why do you think many students feel that social studies is boring?
2. How can teachers help students to be more involved in their communities and world?

Activities

a. Combining the New, Old, and What Will Be

Time: 40–50 minutes
Materials: Newspapers, texts, online sources

The facilitator divides the group into smaller cooperative groups to write local, national, international, sports, or entertainment news articles telling about past, present, and future events. Appropriate grade-level texts, online sites, and available newspapers can be consulted. Encourage everyone to share their thoughts on the positive or negative impact these news events have or had on individuals, communities, nations, civilizations, and societies. Past events can include those from 10 to 1,000 years ago, written from the perspective of that civilization or generation.

b. Social Studies for All Grades and Students

Time: 30 minutes
Materials: Handout 8

Participants choose a grade level from K–12 and one social studies topic, selecting from geography, economics, world history, cultural awareness, or government. The next step is for each person to design an appropriate classroom lesson for the grade level and topic, addressing the inclusive elements as shown on Handout 8. This lesson can be completed individually or in groups, depending upon classroom dynamics, grade levels, and educators' interests. If coteachers are present, encourage the pair to work together. If the facilitator desires, Handout 8 may also be applied to many other subject areas.

c. HPQ (Historical People Quotient): Who Are These People?

Time: 30–40 minutes
Materials: *More Inclusion Strategies That Work! Aligning Student Strengths With Standards* (page 179, Figure 9.6), appropriate research materials

Participants are divided into trios or quartets to write two facts about each of the people in Figure 9.6 within a 20-minute time frame. Afterward, the answers are collectively shared. For an extended activity, participants cooperatively write a script with a cast that includes some of these historical characters. Encourage participants to turnkey this social studies script writing with their own students for interdisciplinary connections.

Self-Reflection and Journal Writing Prompts

How can educators help learners *experience the past* or understand more about foreign countries and cultures they never visited or places or people about which students have limited prior knowledge? What do you remember about your favorite social studies lesson as a student? Are social studies textbooks sensitive to other cultures, or do they need to be more reflective of a global society?

Resources for Extending Your Learning

Content Standards for Social Studies. http://www.ncss.org. Developed by the National Council for the Social Studies (NCSS).

Globalization & Education. http://globalizationandeducation.ed.uiuc.edu

Scholastic Magazines for High Schools. http://teacher.scholastic .com/products/classmags/highschool.htm (*The New York Times Upfront*: Grades 9–12, Social Studies/Journalism; *Teaching Tolerance Magazine*, published by the Southern Poverty Law Center, http://www.tolerance.org/teach/resources/index.jsp). Subscription is free, but registration is required.

Chapter 10. Standards-Based Art, Dance, Theater, and Music Objectives

Summary With Practical Applications

The arts cannot be categorized as superfluous content areas, and they certainly do not fall into a "sprinkles on the learning" category. Being successful in academic subjects involves many skills that the arts contain and propagate, such as self-discipline, practice, perseverance, attention to detail, good listening skills, understanding patterns and systems of notation, planning, communicating, interpreting, evaluating, and learning about other cultures and societies. Creating scripts, choreographing physical movements, hearing tempos and beats, and creating sounds with voices and instruments allow students avenues of creativity and connections to other disciplines. Brain-based learning advocates maintain that the arts can fuel learning and allow students necessary emotional releases. Most important, the arts are excellent alternate avenues of expression, instruction, assessment, creativity, and enjoyment. The arts have an integral place in all classrooms. A student who may dislike reading but likes to act, sing, or dance can very well shine in an inclusive classroom.

Discussion Questions

1. Why are the arts and extracurricular activities often the first budgets to be reduced in school districts?
2. Do you agree or disagree that the mastery of the arts can very well connect to student improvements in the *3Rs* of reading, writing, and arithmetic?
3. How can learning about the arts help students understand more about other civilizations, cultures, societies, and themselves?

Activities

• *a. Art-Filled Dancing Curriculum Jingles*

Time: 50 minutes
Materials: Curriculum texts, online curriculum sites, *More Inclusion Strategies That Work! Aligning Student Strengths With*

Standards (pages 87–237). Other appropriate manipulatives include sound effects, markers, crayons, poster paper, props, and scenery.

The facilitator divides the group according to birth months, for example, January–March, April–June, July–September, and October–December. Each group is then instructed to review Part II of *More Inclusion Strategies That Work!* to pick a curriculum topic to demonstrate with a dance, song, background sounds, accompanying visuals, props, and/or scenery. Their artful presentation can range from a skit to a score, dance ensemble, and more by choreographing dance steps, emotively creating curriculum jingles, drawing scenery, creating handheld props and signs, and playing commercial or self-created instruments. The idea is to expressively demonstrate the concepts through the lyrics, beats, rhythms, tones, tempos, pitches, voices, patterns, instruments, sound effects, movements, and art.

Self-Reflection and Journal Writing Prompts

What effect does music have on your mood? Do you find yourself unconsciously moving about or humming a song during longer sitting periods? Why do some students know the lyrics to their favorite songs but can't remember specific curriculum facts? Do you like listening to music with headphones or your MP3 player while exercising? Do you ever *picture* what someone is saying?

Resources for Extending Your Learning

Edwards, B. (1999). *The new drawing on the right side of the brain.* New York: Tarcher/Penguin. http://www.drawright.com.
The Kennedy Center ArtsEdge. http://artsedge.kennedy-center.org.
Music Educators National Conference (MENC). The National Association for Music Education at http://www.menc.org.
Sacks, O. (2007). *Musicophilia: Tales of music and the brain.* New York: Knopf.
Songs for Teaching: Using Music to Promote Learning. http://songsforteaching.com.

Chapter 11. Standards-Based Health/Physical Education Objectives

Summary With Practical Applications

Healthy behavior includes guiding students to make positive choices with nutrition, exercise, and hygiene. It involves strength training, daily diets, teamwork, responsibility, and safety. Students with attention, behavioral, social, emotional, physical, sensory, and learning issues benefit from following healthy routines. Students with physical differences also need to be challenged to maximize their potentials, without always diluting the activity, or assuming that no elements of a given physical task can be accomplished. In addition, direct skill instruction for improved physical education begins in classrooms that outline and advocate healthy lifestyles in terms of sensible daily personal choices, such as exercise and nutrition routines. Modeling and teaching these lifetime concepts and skills assists students with self-esteem issues, depression, personality differences, and those students with varying perceptual, physical, and cognitive needs. Regular exercise routines or even simple *brain breaks* may proactively squash outbursts by allowing students active options in given space and boundaries. Flexibility, perseverance, learning to cooperate with others, and making good personal decisions need to be acknowledged through movements, both fine and gross motor ones. Direct skill instruction about drugs and alcohol is also crucial in the earlier formative ages, before students enter the somewhat turbulent teen years. Physical education definitely involves strength training for both the body and mind.

Discussion Questions

1. Why are athletes so loved by children and set up as their role models, as opposed to students valuing Pulitzer Prize winners or great mathematicians?
2. Do you agree that healthy bodies lead to healthy minds?
3. Do you have a regular daily or weekly exercise routine?
4. Why do you think obesity has become a growing concern for young children, adolescents, and adults? What can educators do to address this health concern?

Activities

a. Following Directions

Time: 5–10 minutes
Materials: Overhead 2

The facilitator points to directions on the compass rose on Overhead 2 as participants stand and stretch their arms to that same direction of either north, south, east, or west. The group also says the directions the facilitator points to, and then follows more complex intermittent ones, such as northeast, southwest, and so on. As participants follow along, the directions are varied, such as saying the direction east or right, then pointing to the opposite direction of west or left or vocalizing the opposite to check for listening skills and attention to details. Excellent *brain break* for students in inclusive classrooms or adults sitting too long during lectures.

- *b. Yo-Yo Dieting and Healthy Choices*

Time: 30 minutes

Facilitator invites participants to think of positive, neutral, and negative statements about personal health choices and the resulting consequences for themselves or other individuals they know. Examples can include not sleeping enough and feeling tired, being anxious and having an upset stomach, not eating enough and feeling dizzy, having too much alcohol to drink and developing a headache, feeling stressed and doing yoga to relax, and more. After group responses are shared, have *healthy discussions* about how these different choices translate into the classroom and impact students and adults.

- *c. I Can Do This, Too!*

Time: 20 minutes
Materials: Handout 9

The group reviews Handout 9 to think of appropriate accommodations and modifications for students with varying physical/learning/sensory needs during classroom and sports activities. Participants select responses from the word choices or add their own ideas. The facilitator invites the group to first consider leaving the activity or skill intact, without major modifications of the objective, allowing the student to perhaps board *a different vehicle* to reach a *comparable destination*. After about 10 minutes, the class shares ideas on how students with varying needs can accomplish the skills and activities.

Self-Reflection and Journal Writing Prompts

Did you ever feel that your lack of physical strength stopped you from accomplishing something? Why do most students, when asked, usually respond that gym is their favorite subject? How does your mood or thoughts at times affect your body?

Resources for Extending Your Learning

Moving and Learning: The Movement Education Specialists. http://www.movingandlearning.com/Resources/SupplementalBooks.htm.
National Standards for Physical Education—American Alliance for Health, Physical Education, Recreation and Dance. http://www.aahperd.org.
Sports for Children with Special Needs. http://specialchildren.about.com/od/specialneedssports.

Chapter 12. Standards-Based Career Education and Life Skills Objectives

Summary With Practical Applications

When students connect school with life, the learning becomes theirs forever! Sometimes, when legislators direct administrators and educators to concentrate solely on high academic performances, the importance of direct skill instruction for everyday living skills and career connections is unduly minimized. The learning definitely needs to be grounded in real-life applications as shown with this chapter's activities.

Discussion Questions

1. Have you always known what you wanted to be when you grew up?
2. Why do some students think that the subjects they are learning about are a waste of time, in terms of their future lives?
3. Is it possible for educators to connect the standards with their neighborhoods and communities?

Activities

● *a. My SIG Profile*

Time: 15 minutes
Materials: *More Inclusion Strategies That Work! Aligning Student Strengths With Standards* (page 224, Figure 12.2)

Using the guidelines from Figure 12.2 or a sheet of paper vertically folded into three columns with the headings S, I, and G, the facilitator directs each participant to introspectively list his or her strengths, interests, and future goals. Afterward, the facilitator invites the participants to TTYP (Talk to Your Peer or Partner) to discover if there is a match or correlation among what each person likes to do, what each person is good at, and what each person hopes to accomplish. After pairs share, and if time permits, the class can reflect on this activity as a whole, thinking about how students sometimes have strengths, interests, and goals that do not always match their present needs, situations, or requirements at school or at home.

● *b. Neighborhood Connections*

Time: 30 minutes
Materials: Yellow Pages of neighborhood businesses or online sites of community business listings, e-mail program, phones, and/or postage stamps and materials to write letters; Handout 10

The facilitator invites the group to thumb through the Yellow Pages, either online or hard copies, to compile a list of different community businesses that would be appropriate ones to contact (Handout 10). The group is subdivided according to grade level, population, or academic subject. The purpose is to tap into community resources to motivate students to close the gap between the subjects learned in school and neighborhood opportunities and future career possibilities. Once the list is compiled, now or at a future session or time, contact the businesses by phone, e-mail, or in writing to solidify guest speakers visiting the school or to arrange on-site field trips.

c. If They Could Shop, What the Subjects Would Buy

Time: 30 minutes
Materials: Creative minds

The facilitator invites the group to imagine that different subjects were let loose in a shopping mall and had a $500 budget to spend. Where would they shop? What would they buy and why? The group is divided into *teams of shoppers* to creatively plan their shopping excursion for *subjective consumer education.*

Self-Reflection and Journal Writing Prompts

How can you as a teacher better prepare your students with the knowledge and skills they need to be productive and contributing members of society? If you could alter an aspect of your career, what would you change? Why do functional life skills need to be addressed in both school and home environments?

Resources for Extending Your Learning

Getting Real Program for functional academics at http://www
.nprinc.com/spec_edu/grpm.htm.
Life Skills Training. http://www.lifeskillstraining.com.
Mooney, J., & Cole, D. (2000). *Learning outside the lines.* New York: Fireside.

Chapter 13. Standards-Based Social/Behavioral/Emotional Objectives

Summary With Practical Applications

It is often said that children will remember how you treated them, long after they forget what you taught them. When students are in accepting and unthreatening classroom environments, they are willing to face challenges and take risks to *tread on new academic territory.* A social climate that allows students to be an integral part of the lesson without fearing failure, rejection, or exclusion speaks volumes in terms of both social and academic growth. If students feel good about themselves, this higher self-esteem will give them inner strength and increased self-confidence. Students with behavioral, emotional, or social issues need direct skill instruction on ways to handle both their own moods and interpersonal relationships. Also, teachers must remember to keep track of the quieter students as well, who do not demand the extra attention, but who may be silently crying out. Even though students are physically included, very often they are emotionally withdrawn or self-excluded from school dynamics, shying away from uncomfortable situations. Not all students have supportive home environments, or adults who model appropriate behaviors. Reaching students with differences means that you need to reach all parts of students, from their brains to their hearts. Cooperative learning, realistic praise, increased metacognition, self-advocacy, direct skill instruction, modeling, and, most important, guided and monitored interactions with peers in inclusive settings afford students the opportunities they need to succeed in the classroom and well beyond into the world with their coworkers, neighbors, life partners, and socially healthy children of their own.

Discussion Questions

1. Why is transforming the letters in the word *how* to the word *who* a vital inclusive ingredient?
2. Think of an awkward social situation you experienced as a student. Would you like to return to it and handle it differently with your adult hindsight?
3. Why do some students feel the need to bully other students?
4. What can teachers do to circumvent some of the peer pressure students experience in school settings?
5. Why do some students in inclusive classrooms prefer to act out or misbehave rather than admit that they do not understand the lesson?

Activities

a. The Labyrinth: Working Backward—FBAs

Time: 30 minutes
Materials: Handout 11

The facilitator reminds the group that most classroom behavior occurs for a reason. Punishments such as reporting to the principal's office for detention or extra assignments do not address the cause of the behavior and will only temporarily control the visible surface symptoms. Teachers need to observe, record, document, and think of viable solutions that reach the root of problem behavior. Invite participants to review and discuss emotions via a roundtable discussion, telling if they agree or disagree with certain statements. The group then shares realistic situations (no names, please) in which they have witnessed behaviors that most likely occurred for the listed reasons on Handout 11.

Self-Reflection and Journal Writing Prompts

Why do some students or adults just go along with the crowd, afraid to voice a differing viewpoint for fear of ridicule or rejection? Can social skills be taught? Describe a situation where words said one thing, but the body language spoke quite differently.

Resources for Extending Your Learning

Baker, J. (2006). *The social skills picture book for high school and beyond.* Arlington, TX: Future Horizons.

Cooperative Learning Network: Social Skills. http://home.att.net/~clnetwork/socialsk.htm.

Council for Children with Behavioral Disorders (Division of Council for Exceptional Children). http://www.ccbd.net.

Creative Therapy Associates—Mood Dudes/Feelings Posters. http://www.ctherapy.com.

Dr. Mac's Amazing Behavior Management Site. http://www.behavioradvisor.com.

Illinois Learning Standards. http://www.isbe.state.il.us/ils/social_emotional/standards.htm.

School-Connect: Optimizing the High School Experience. http://www.school-connect.net.

Part III. Application of Strengths and Standards to Inclusive Environments

Chapter 14. Standards-Based Interdisciplinary/Cross-Curricular Lessons

Summary With Practical Applications

Whether teachers have classes of students who prefer to listen to Mozart, the Beatles, or Kanye West, the lessons need to be memorable, motivating, multidisciplinary, and applicable ones. Interdisciplinary lessons allow students to see the whole picture while mastering individual skills. Quite often, many academic skills are embedded in the activities without the students even knowing. Meaningful connections, relevant to students' lives, are both fun to teach and fun to learn! Interdisciplinary primary, intermediate, and secondary lessons honor the subjects and students' interests in ways that challenge abilities and acknowledge the curriculum standards for all learners while inviting learners to be constructive and active students.

Discussion Questions

1. Describe learning situations that connect multiple intelligences with multiple subjects.
2. Should school districts allot teachers more collaboration time to plan multidisciplinary units, for example, district workshops, preps, faculty meetings?

Activities

● *a. Interdisciplinary Connections for All Seasons*

Time: 30–40 minutes
Materials: Overhead 3

The facilitator demonstrates the following lesson by asking the group to think about seasons in different locations, for example, summer in Jerusalem, spring in Vietnam, fall in Vermont, winter in Switzerland. Invite suggestions of other locations from the group and how the subjects can be explored using the concept of seasons in different locations. To allow for practical classroom applications, turn Overhead 3 into a handout and invite the participants to individually or cooperatively think of upcoming lessons or past curriculum concepts they have taught and interdisciplinary ways to *toss the learning together*!

Self-Reflection and Journal Writing Prompts

● *b. Trading Places*

Think back on a lesson you taught and trade places with one of your students. Write a journal entry from the student's point of view telling whether he or she thought it was an exciting or boring lesson, giving an honest student perspective. Tell how you plan to better connect the subjects with each other and with students' lives.

Resources for Extending Your Learning

Jenkins, R. (2005, May/June). Interdisciplinary instruction in the inclusion classroom. *Teaching Exceptional Children, 27,* 5.
Lesson Plans 4 Teachers. http://www.lessonplans4teachers.com/inter disciplinary.php.
Teachnology. http://teach-nology.com/teachers/lesson_plans/inter disciplinary.

Chapter 15. Attaining Inclusion

Summary With Practical Applications

Inclusion is not a specific program that can be implemented the same way for all students, since the variability of the student population demands alternate approaches to best meet each individual student's needs. Preplanning lessons that align with individual educational programs means that the necessary accommodations and modifications maximize students' potentials with proactive universal designs. At times, inclusion involves dissecting the classroom levels with baseline knowledge standards, advancing levels, and more challenging assignments. Invite the group to think of their own curriculum objective they want their students to achieve, as shown in Figure 15.2 on page 286. Encourage participants to review the baseline knowledge standards, advancing levels, more challenging assignments, and possible accommodations listed in Part II for differing curriculum areas.

Discussion Questions

1. Is an inclusive environment the appropriate placement for all students?
2. What preparation and administrative support do teachers in general education classrooms need to help learners with special needs?
3. What does it mean to be a *team player*?

Activities

● *a. CPR for Inclusion*

Time: 10–15 minutes
Materials: *More Inclusion Strategies That Work! Aligning Student Strengths With Standards* (page 285, Figure 15.1)

The facilitator asks students to review the *CPR for Inclusion* table on page 285 to fill in the sentences on pages 285–286: *Inclusion can be successful when* _____. *I still wonder if* _____. *One day* _____. After about 5 minutes of independent writing, the facilitator invites participants to share their responses in a round-robin fashion for further group discussion on ways to implement inclusive practices.

● *b. Inclusive Collaborations and Celebrations: Olympic Rings*

Time: 20–30 minutes
Materials: Teacher-constructed medals

The group divides into trios to describe hypothetical people in inclusion scenarios who win gold, silver, and bronze medals for classroom inclusion achievements.

c. Administrative Dilemmas

Time: 20–30 minutes
Materials: *More Inclusion Strategies That Work! Aligning Student Strengths With Standards* (pages 290–294)

The facilitator asks the group for *frustrated thespian* volunteers, willing to act out one of the following roles in the two administrative scripts: Narrator, Principal, Ms. Objection, Mr. C. Sense, and Ms. Whatta Future. After both scripts are read, the whole group answers the 9 questions in Figure 15.3 on page 294 to compare and contrast the two different faculty meetings.

Self-Reflection and Journal Writing Prompts

Review Figures 15.5 and 15.6 and how documenting progress is an essential inclusive ingredient. Which modifications or accommodations are the most difficult or simplest to implement? Name some additional modifications that you think are imperative ones.

Resources for Extending Your Learning

Klein, S., & Schive, K. (2001). *You will dream new dreams: Inspirational stories by parents of students with disabilities.* New York: Kensington Books.
National Staff Development Council. http://www.nsdc.org.

Chapter 16. Rewards for All

Summary With Practical Applications

Everyone is a major stakeholder when students with special needs achieve academic and social gains in inclusive classrooms. General and special educators, related staff, administrators, peers with and without special needs, families of all students, and society as a whole are the inclusive winners. Educators who honor students' strengths deliver curriculum standards on levels that allow students to be successful, regardless of the variables presented. Holding high expectations for all learners yields beneficial rewards!

Discussion Questions

1. Why has the pendulum shifted for students with special needs, from being educated in separate classrooms to inclusive environments? Do you think that this is a trend, or is inclusion here to stay?

2. How can educators collaborate more with families to achieve higher results for students with special needs?

3. Who in society stands to gain the most from inclusive education? How can classroom teachers be better prepared to accomplish more inclusive successes?

Activities

a. How Much Do You Remember?

Time: 20–30 minutes
Materials: Handout 12

The facilitator invites participants to answer questions a–y on Handout 12 by reviewing the given pages in *More Inclusion Strategies That Work! Aligning Student Strengths With Standards*. Participants can work in cooperative groups or individually to record written answers. Some of the questions certainly have more than one correct answer and are specifically designed to spark more communication and collaboration about effective inclusion strategies.

b. Inclusion Roundtable Discussion

Time: 20 minutes
Materials: Handout 13

The facilitator divides the group into cooperative subgroups of five people who simultaneously respond to each of the roundtable prompts of a–e. Afterward, the group shares the inclusion comments by passing the written responses *around the table.*

Self-Reflection and Journal Writing Prompts

Invite participants to divide a journal page into three vertical columns, heading the first column with a heart for listing what they love about inclusion, the second column with a question mark for things about inclusion that they are uncertain about, and the third one with a star for inclusion points that they believe are the most vital ingredients.

To Sum It Up

More Inclusion Strategies That Work! Aligning Student Strengths With Standards, is filled with excellent strategies that look great on paper, yet if they are not consistently applied in inclusive classrooms on a daily basis, they are all ineffective ones. Something is good as long as it is useful, and that goes for effective inclusion strategies too! Good luck with your arduous, continuous, collaborative, and incredible inclusive efforts!

Resources for Extending Your Learning

Gerlach, K. (2004). *Let's team up! A checklist for paraeducators, teachers, and principals.* Washington, DC: NEA Professional Library.

Karten, T. (2005). *Inclusion strategies that work! Research-based methods for the classroom.* Thousand Oaks, CA: Corwin Press.

Karten, T. (2007). *Inclusion activities that work! Grades K–2, 3–5, 6–8.* Thousand Oaks, CA: Corwin Press.

Karten, T. (2008). *Embracing disabilities in the classroom: Strategies to maximize students' assets.* Thousand Oaks, CA: Corwin Press.

Thousand, J., Villa, R., & Nevin, A. (2007). *Differentiated instruction: Collaborative planning and teaching for universally designed learning.* Thousand Oaks, CA: Corwin Press.

Tomlinson, C., & McTighe, J. (2006). *Integrating differentiated instruction and understanding by design: Connecting content and kids.* Alexandria, VA: Association for Supervision and Curriculum Development.

Handouts

Handout 1. A–Z Inclusive Assessment Rubric

Directions

Place the letters where you think they belong in reference to instruction and assessments. When the group reviews the chart together, adjust as desired.

Excellent Inclusive Practices	Good Inclusive Practices	Fair Inclusive Practices	Noninclusive Practices

a. Expectations are high for all students

b. Thinks students with lower skills do not belong in the same classroom as those students with higher skills

c. Instruction is test-oriented

d. Instruction is student-oriented

e. Illustrations/literary works by artists/ writers from different cultures/ disabilities are included

f. Good grades are the bottom line

g. Classroom occasionally includes cooperative learning

h. Students do not keep profiles of their progress

i. Grading is multipurpose

j. Tests are never weighted

k. Tests are always weighted

l. Testing is frequent

m. Same test format is given throughout the year

n. Portfolios are used for students with highest abilities

o. Response time is monitored and limited

p. Will orally read and explain test directions

q. Critical thinking skill questions are required only for students without IEPs

r. It's all about students achieving higher grades

s. Team-building is valued

t. Assessments are diagnostic, formative, and summative

u. Standards are valued

v. Authoritative classroom

w. Testing includes efforts and progress as well as achievement

x. Families are not given input

y. Limited challenges given to those with the most needs

z. Other idea of what constitutes excellent inclusive practices

Handout 2. Smart Chart

Directions

Which intelligence matches the strengths of the people listed on page 39? Correctly place the letters in these slots to achieve a *Smart Chart*.

	S	M	A	R	T
Logical/Mathematical					
Musical/Rhythmic					
Visual/Spatial					
Bodily/Kinesthetic					
Verbal/Linguistic					
Intrapersonal					
Interpersonal					
Existential					
Naturalist					

a. Albert Einstein	b. Student with autism who loves to draw	c. Maya Angelo	d. Martin Luther King	e. Student with dyscalculia who dances	f. Sigmund Freud
g. Maya Lin	h. Euclid	i. David Letterman	j. Socrates	k. Frida Kahlo	l. Student who classifies cars
m. James Audubon	n. Student with a learning disability who can't spell, but keeps a journal	o. Andrea Bocelli	p. Public speaker with a physical disability	q. Student with dyslexia who is an excellent doodler	r. Student who cannot read well, but is always inquisitive
s. Student with behavioral issues who plays the saxophone	t. Student who is not good at listening, but is an excellent team player	u. Vincent van Gogh	v. Student who learns well with graphic organizers	w. Spiderman	x. Stephen Hawking
y. Your own description	y. Your own description	y. Your own description	y. Your own description	y. Your own description	y. Your own description

Handout 3. Looking Back to Move Ahead

The topic I am comparing and contrasting is _____

_____.

Directions

Think about how you learned about this topic and then compare and contrast your prior and current knowledge. Decide in which circle you would place the words in the table below. If the words belong in both circles, then put them in the overlapping or linking one. As an option, think of a student you tried to teach a given concept to instead.

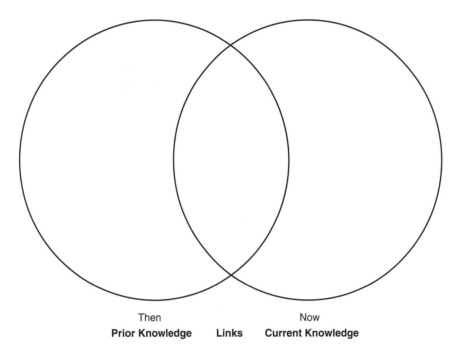

Then   Now
Prior Knowledge   **Links**   **Current Knowledge**

Decide in which circle you would place some of the following words. Add your own, too!

mastery	review	repetition	perseverance	research
textbooks	modeling	peer assistance	cooperative learning	patience
regression	frustration	communication	inquiry	metacognition
sadness	joy	optimism	pessimism	connections
movement	role-playing	time	growth	patterns

Handout 4. Strategies People Search

Strategy Number	Classroom Application/Scenario
1	
2	
3	
4	
5	
6	
7	
8	
9	
10	
11	
12	
13	
14	
15	
16	
17	
18	

Group Name:

Participants:

Handout 5. Problem Solving: Inclusive Strategies

Directions

Decide which strategy you will apply to solve the following problems, from the choices in Figure 7.8 on page 134 in *More Inclusion Strategies That Work! Aligning Student Strengths With Standards*. Determine relevant and irrelevant information and whether or not more than one strategy or approach could be used to solve each of these problems. Show all work on separate scrap paper. On the reverse side of the paper, list interest-generated word problem topics for the population you instruct and some strategies you would employ to guide students toward solutions, and then create a few of your own!

1. Special, General, Friendly, and Smarty prepared for their upcoming chemistry final. Special studied 5 more hours than Smarty. General studied 3 hours less than Friendly, while Special studied 3 times as much as General. If Friendly studied a total of 5 hours, how many hours did each of these students study for the test?

2. Ms. Perfect designed a 25-question test for her math class on multiplication and division computations and properties. Five of the questions on the order of operations were multiple choice, 12 multiplication and division problems were free response, and the remaining were word problems. Identify the percentages, decimals, and fractions of the whole test for each type of problem.

3. Mr. Helper, who coteaches with Ms. Perfect, marked the above math test and discovered that 4 of the 5 students who were receiving in-class support achieved grades of 80% or better. Eighty-six percent of the students who were not classified received grades of 80% or better as well. If there were 35 students in the whole class, approximately how many students achieved grades of 80% or better?

4. The fifth grade was planning a field trip to the Liberty Science Center in Jersey City. If the five classes had 28, 27, 29, 33, and 31 students attending the trip with 7 teachers and 8 other adult chaperones, about how many buses were needed, if each bus had room to seat 50 people?

5. On back-to-school night, parents and families attended sessions given by Mr. Fungi, Mr. Boring, Ms. Downer, and Mrs. Smiley. Mr. Fungi had 4 times as many in attendance as Mr. Boring. If Mr. Fungi had 32 parents in attendance, and Ms. Downer had half as many as Mr. Boring, and the total number of family members in attendance was 75, how many family members attended each teacher's back-to-school-night sessions?

Handout 6. The Goal of Special Education

Directions

Solve each mathematical problem and place the correct letter above each blank. Numbered answers correspond to the order of the letters in the alphabet as shown in the code below. Try to think of different mathematical problems, without duplicating the ones on this page, to complete the rest of the sentence. The message reveals the goal of *special* education.

T	O							
5×4	$12 + 3$	$32 \div 2$	6×3	$60 \div 12$	4×4	$10 \div 10$	9×2	$30 \div 6$

$9 \div 3$	$16 \div 2$	3×3	$9 + 3$	$20 - 16$	$36 \div 2$	$40 \div 8$	2×7	10×2

$30 \div 2$	3×4	5×1	$18 \div 18$	$-5 + 9$

8×2	$12 + 6$	3×5	$-8 + 12$	$63 \div 3$	$27 \div 9$	10×2	$54 \div 6$	11×2	$3 + 2$

$63 \div 7$	$30 - 16$	🕐	$3 + 2$	$9 \times 2 - 2$	$12 \div 2 - 1$	7×2

$100 \div 25$	$100 \div 20$	$9 + 5$	$1,000 \div 50$

L	I	V	E	S	A	S
_	_	_	_	_	_	_

M	E	M	B	E	R	S
_	_	_	_	_	_	_

O	F	T	H	E	A	D	U	L	T
_	_	_	_	_	_	_	_	_	_

C	O	M	M	U	N	I	T	Y.
_	_	_	_	_	_	_	_	_

A	B	C	D	E	F	G	H	I	J	K	L	M	N	O	P	Q	R	S	T	U	V	W	X	Y	Z
1	2	3	4	5	6	7	8	9	10	11	12	13	14	15	16	17	18	19	20	21	22	23	24	25	26

SOURCE: Adapted from Karten, T. (2004). *Inclusion strategies that work! Research-based methods for the classroom.* Thousand Oaks, CA: Corwin Press.

Handout 7. Science Levels and Accommodations for All Students Planner

Directions

Cooperative groups jigsaw this chart, to satisfy the headings of each row with different objectives and learner accommodations for one science concept. Each group can cooperatively review the appropriate sections from *More Inclusion Strategies That Work! Aligning Student Strengths With Standards*, pages 143–168, for more information about the standards, strategies, and appropriate accommodations. Groups demonstrate their lessons and share their findings to allow the whole group to gain ideas on possible ways to differentiate lessons for students with varying levels and needs for these science topics.

Word/Concept/ Content Area/ Specific Curriculum Standard	Description/ Vocabulary/ Objective/ Lesson/ Procedure/ Assessment	Baseline Knowledge	Advancing Level	More Challenging Assignments	Accommodations/ Modifications for Students With . . .
1. Shadows					
2. Scientific inquiry					
3. Chemical/ physical changes					
4. Classification					
5. Cell structure					
6. Physics					
7. Gravity					
8. Condensation					
9. Astronomy					
10. Weathering					
11. Technology					

Handout 8. Lesson Plan

Topic: _____

_____

Lesson Concept: _____

_____

Objective: _____

_____

Desired Goals (Social/Academic/Emotional/Behavioral/Social/Physical/Cognitive):

_____

_____

Baseline Knowledge: _____

_____

Motivating Activity: _____

_____

Visual/Auditory/Kinesthetic/Tactile: _____

_____

Sensory Elements: _____

_____

Critical/Creative Thinking Skills: _____

_____

Interpersonal Activity/Cooperative Roles: _____

_____

(Continued)

(Continued)

Curriculum Connections: _____

_____

Possible Accommodations: _____

_____

Parallel Activity: _____

_____

Anticipated Roles of Coteachers/Staff/Students/Family:

General Educator: _____

_____

Special Educator: _____

_____

Instructional Assistant: _____

_____

Student: _____

_____

Peers/Family/Specialists/Related Services/Administration: _____

_____

Adult/Peer/Self-Assessments: _____

_____

Closure: _____

_____

Revisitation Dates: _____

_____

SOURCE: Adapted from Karten, T. (2004). *Inclusion strategies that work! Research-based methods for the classroom.* Thousand Oaks, CA: Corwin Press.

Handout 9. I Can Do This, Too!

Student With . . .	Skill/Activity	Accommodations Modifications Parallel Assignments
shorter stature	basketball	
using a wheelchair	playing volleyball	
limited vision	using a microscope	
deafness	listening to a lecture	
cerebral palsy	handwriting assignment	
one arm	archery	
dystonia (uncontrollable movements)	navigating sites on a computer	
asthma	recess outside	
blindness	art activity	
speech disorder	oral presentation	
stress or anxiety	taking a standardized test	

Some Factors to Consider

safety

flexibility

distance

time

peers

breaks

assistance/accommodations/ modifications/scaffolding

size/shape of equipment

different or additional materials

weight/height

modeling

repetition

effort

progress

emotions

altering expectations

Handout 10. Neighborhood Connections and Objectives

Directions

Compile a list of appropriate businesses/community resources to (a) invite guest speakers for on-site school visits and (b) arrange class field trips.

Math Objective

Business Name: _____

Contact: _____ Hours of Operation: _____

Address: _____

E-Mail: _____ Phone: _____

Science Objective

Business Name: _____

Contact: _____ Hours of Operation: _____

Address: _____

E-Mail: _____ Phone: _____

Social Studies Objective

Business Name: _____

Contact: _____ Hours of Operation: _____

Address: _____

E-Mail: _____ Phone: _____

Language Arts Objective

Business Name: _____

Contact: _____ Hours of Operation: _____

Address: _____

E-Mail: _____ Phone: _____

Physical Education Objective

Business Name: _____

Contact: _____ Hours of Operation: _____

Address: _____

E-Mail: _____ Phone: _____

Art Objective

Business Name: _____

Contact: _____ Hours of Operation: _____

Address: _____

E-Mail: _____ Phone: _____

Music Objective

Business Name: _____

Contact: _____ Hours of Operation: _____

Address: _____

E-Mail: _____ Phone: _____

Communication/World Languages Objective

Business Name: _____

Contact: _____ Hours of Operation: _____

Address: _____

E-Mail: _____ Phone: _____

Subject _____ Objective

Business Name: _____

Contact: _____ Hours of Operation: _____

Address: _____

E-Mail: _____ Phone: _____

Handout 11. Working Backward

Functional Behavioral Assessment

Fill in your ideas for what we as educators can do to circumvent inappropriate behavioral reoccurrences

Underlying Reasons	Describe Hypothetical Students and Possible Connective Classroom Scenarios
I never learned how to do this before!	
I want more attention!	
I hope to escape or avoid the assignment!	
It's boring. I know this stuff already!	
These rules are just not important!	
Other reason:	

Handout 12. How Much Do You Remember?

Directions

Try to answer as many questions as possible under the "shapely" categories, and then check the page numbers listed for the answers. Work cooperatively, collectively, in game format, or solo.

Is It About Cognitive, Perceptual, Behavioral, Social, Emotional, Communicative, Physical, and/or Learning Levels?

Answers on page 58 in More Inclusion Strategies That Work! Aligning Student Strengths With Standards; *some descriptors have more than one connection.*

a. Shy student, will not participate.

b. Student cannot verbalize misunderstandings.

c. Visual and auditory confusions interfere with the learning.

d. Student is strictly a concrete learner.

e. Prior frustrating experiences have soured this student on academics.

Name Applicable Accommodations for Each Description

Answers found in Part II.

f. Student needs more help with inferential reading skills.

g. Student has difficulty understanding directions in noisy settings.

h. Student is not fond of sitting still for long classroom lectures.

i. Student views fine motor tasks as challenging.

j. Student thinks that the work is too easy

Student Strengths

Answers found on pages 6–24. Respond in people-first language, for example, "student with _____," telling which disability may have each of the described strengths.

k. Student loves routines, tactile elements and pictures, and focused interests.

l. Student likes stories on tape, is motivated to achieve, and has good oral comprehension.

m. Student responds to challenging assignments at accelerated paces.

(Continued)

(Continued)

    n. Student has untapped strengths, likes multisensory and step-by-step approaches.

    o. Student has strong goals, is an independent thinker, and is able to follow consistent rules.

Match the Verbs With the Standards and Subjects

Answers in Part II figures/tables, on pages with content area objectives.

    p. Hypothesize, observe, evaluate

    q. Decode, encode, comprehend

    r. Estimate, compute, reason

    s. Research, debate, connect, compare, contrast

    t. Communicate, express, listen

Major Players Involved

Possible answers found on pages 69–75. Hint: All inclusive players are home and school collaborators!

    u. Increased metacognition is imperative for these individuals.

    v. Understanding ones will schedule common planning time.

    w. These people are on the same classroom page and stage.

    x. People in this environment need to be in the loop, too.

    y. What all *major inclusive players* need to consistently do

Handout 13. Roundtable Discussion

Directions

This activity is a cooperative learning strategy—the roundtable. It quickly allows for the simultaneous sharing of knowledge or opinions on varying topics and content areas through written prompts. In groups of five, each person writes the letter of a different prompt on his or her paper (a–e), briefly responds, and then exchanges papers with someone else in his or her group. Each person then writes comments on another letter prompt, passing the questions around the table until all five people in each group have responded to each prompt. Written comments on individual headings can then be collected for review, or orally shared in class discussion.

Roundtable Statements

a. Students in inclusive settings achieve high academic skills.

b. Teachers can address the strengths of learners in inclusive classrooms.

c. Staff and family attitudes about inclusion vary.

d. Without collaboration, inclusion is impossible.

e. Accommodations and modifications enhance the standards.

Circle one roundtable statement letter prompt. Respond below with comments on the roundtable statement. Names are optional.	a	b	c	d	e

Overheads

Overhead 1. Connecting to Inclusion

T _____

E _____

S _____

T _____

the

G _____

A _____

M _____

E _____

C _____

O _____

R _____

D _____

Overhead 2. Compass Rose

Overhead 3. Interdisciplinary Approach

Educational Salads

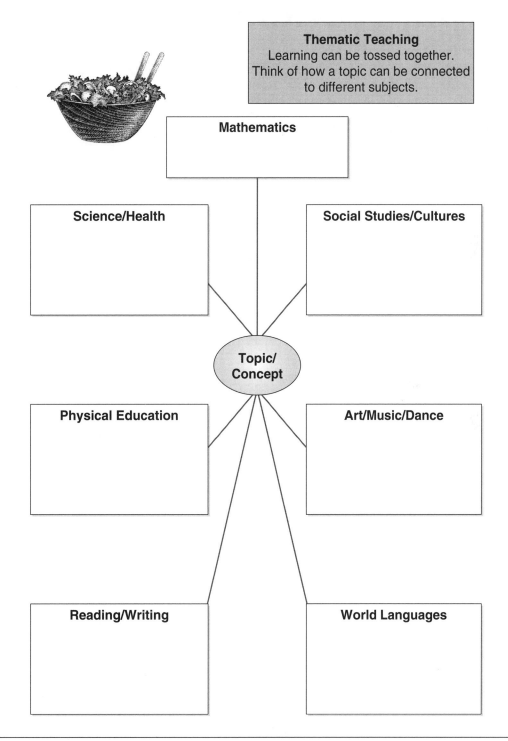

Thematic Teaching
Learning can be tossed together.
Think of how a topic can be connected
to different subjects.

Mathematics

Science/Health

Social Studies/Cultures

Topic/
Concept

Physical Education

Art/Music/Dance

Reading/Writing

World Languages

SOURCE: Adapted from Karten, T. (2004). *Inclusion strategies that work! Research-based methods for the classroom.* Thousand Oaks, CA: Corwin Press.

Sample Workshop Agendas

Half-Day Workshop Agenda

Welcoming Activity

Read "Pledge With an Edge" (Chapter 3b) *(5 minutes)*

Purpose of Workshop (5 minutes)

- Examine how to capitalize upon students' interests, motivations, and strengths.
- Review research in the field about effective inclusion practices.
- Explore content curriculum standards and ways to differentiate objectives.
- Identify baseline, advancing, and more challenging classroom assignments.
- Explore ways to develop critical thinking skills in all learners.
- Apply valuable inclusive practices, strategies, and accommodations.
- Match instructional styles and assessments with students' needs.
- Collaborate with colleagues to reflect upon inclusion implementation.

Activities

1. Discuss whether there is a template for inclusion *(5 minutes)*
2. Band-Aid Activity (Chapter 2a) *(10 minutes)*
3. Stepping Into the Classroom: Best Versus Worst Scenarios (Chapter 1b) *(30 minutes)*
4. How Much Do You Remember? (Chapter 16a) *(20 minutes)*
5. Inclusion PAYS (Chapter 1c) *(30 minutes)*
6. Inclusion Rubric: Appropriate Instructional Strategies and Assessments (Chapter 2c) *(15 minutes)*
7. Good Practices (Chapter 4a) *(20 minutes)*
8. Following Directions (Chapter 11a) *(5–10 minutes)*
9. Note-Taking Acronym: TEST the GAME CORD (Chapter 4c) *(30 minutes)*

10. Connecting the GAME CORD (Chapter 4d) *(20 minutes)*
11. Expanding Upon Inclusion: ED'S CAR (Chapter 6a) *(20 minutes)*

Summary and Evaluation *(10 minutes)*

CPR for Inclusion (Chapter 15a) or Self-Reflection and Journal Writing Prompts (Chapter 16)

One-Day Workshop Agenda

Welcoming Activity

Read "Pledge With an Edge" (Chapter 3b) *(5 minutes)*

Purpose of Workshop *(5 minutes)*

- Examine how to capitalize upon students' interests, motivations, and strengths.
- Review research in the field about effective inclusion practices.
- Explore content curriculum standards and ways to differentiate objectives.
- Identify baseline, advancing, and more challenging classroom assignments.
- Explore ways to develop critical thinking skills in all learners.
- Integrate multiple intelligences in lessons.
- Honor social and emotional inclusive components.
- Apply valuable inclusive practices, strategies, and accommodations.
- Match instructional styles and assessments with students' needs.
- Collaborate with colleagues to plan for inclusion implementation.
- Reflect upon appropriate inclusive practices.

Activities

1. Discuss whether there is a template for inclusion *(5 minutes)*
2. Band-Aid Activity (Chapter 2a) *(10 minutes)*
3. Inclusion Rubric: Appropriate Instructional Activities and Assessments (Chapter 2c) *(15 minutes)*
4. Expanding Upon Inclusion: ED'S CAR (Chapter 6a) *(20 minutes)*
5. Inclusion PAYS (Chapter 1c) *(20 minutes)*
6. Note-Taking Acronym: TEST the GAME CORD (Chapter 4c) *(20 minutes)*
7. Connecting the GAME CORD (Chapter 4d) *(20 minutes)*
8. The Labyrinth: Working Backward—FBAs (Chapter 13a) *(40 minutes)*

Class Break

9. Good Practices (Chapter 4a) *(20 minutes)*
10. Smart Chart (Chapter 3a) *(10 minutes)*
11. Art-Filled Dancing Curriculum Jingles (Chapter 10a) *(30–40 minutes)*
12. Looking Back to Move Ahead (Chapter 3c) *(20–30 minutes)*
13. Following Directions (Chapter 11a) *(5–10 minutes)*
14. Inclusion Roundtable Discussion (Chapter 16b) *(20 minutes)*
15. Inclusive Collaborations and Celebrations: Olympic Rings (Chapter 15b) or Self-Reflection and Journal Writing Prompts (Chapter 15) *(20 minutes)*

Summary and Evaluation *(20 minutes)*

CPR for Inclusion (Chapter 15a) or Self-Reflection and Journal Writing Prompts (Chapter 16)

Inclusion Poem (Chapter 1d)

Two-Day Workshop Agenda

Welcoming Activity

Read "Pledge With an Edge" (Chapter 3b) *(5 minutes)*

Purpose of Workshop *(5 minutes)*

- Examine how to capitalize upon students' interests, motivations, and strengths.
- Review research in the field.
- Explore content curriculum standards and ways to differentiate objectives.
- Identify baseline, advancing, and more challenging classroom assignments.
- Explore ways to develop critical thinking skills in all learners.
- Integrate multiple intelligences in lessons.
- Honor social and emotional components.
- Provide literacy, science, social studies, and mathematics connections.
- Demonstrate effective interdisciplinary lessons.
- Apply valuable inclusive practices, strategies, and accommodations.
- Match instructional styles and assessments with students' needs.
- Collaborate with colleagues to plan for inclusion implementation.
- Reflect upon appropriate inclusive practices.

First-Day Activities

1. Discuss whether there is a template for inclusion *(5 minutes)*
2. Looking Back to Move Ahead (Chapter 3c) *(20–30 minutes)*
3. Inclusion PAYS (Chapter 1c) *(20 minutes)*
4. Inclusion Rubric: Appropriate Instructional Strategies and Assessments (Chapter 2c) *(15 minutes)*
5. Note-Taking Acronym: TEST the GAME CORD (Chapter 4c) *(20 minutes)*
6. Connecting the GAME CORD (Chapter 4d) *(20–30 minutes)*
7. Following Directions (Chapter 11a) *(5–10 minutes)*
8. Good Practices (Chapter 4a) *(40 minutes)*

Class Break

9. Strategies People Search (Chapter 4b) *(40 minutes)*
10. The Labyrinth: Working Backward—FBAs (Chapter 13a) *(40 minutes)*
11. Interdisciplinary Connections for All Seasons (Chapter 14a) *(30–40 minutes)*

Second-Day Activities

12. SOARing Into Reading (Chapter 5b) *(20–30 minutes)*
13. Social Studies for All Grades and Students (Chapter 9b) or Science Levels and Accommodations for All Students (Chapter 8a) *(30 minutes)*
14. If They Could Shop, What the Subjects Would Buy (Chapter 12c) *(30 minutes)*
15. How Much Do You Remember? (Chapter 16a) *(20 minutes)*
16. Art-Filled Dancing Curriculum Jingles (Chapter 10a) *(50 minutes)*

Class Break

17. Expanding Upon Inclusion: ED'S CAR (Chapter 6a) *(20–30 minutes)*
18. I Can Do This, Too! (Chapter 11c) *(20–30 minutes)*
19. Smart Chart (Chapter 3a) *(10–15 minutes)*
20. Inclusive Collaborations and Celebrations: Olympic Rings (Chapter 15b) or Self-Reflection and Journal Writing Prompts (Chapter 15) *(20 minutes)*
21. Inclusion Poem (Chapter 1d) *(5 minutes)*

Summary and Evaluation *(30–40 minutes)*

CPR for Inclusion (Chapter 15a)

Inclusion Roundtable Discussion (Chapter 16b)

Workshop Evaluation Form

Content

- How well did the seminar meet the goals and objectives?

- What professional support will you need to implement what you have learned from this seminar?

- How well did the topics explored in this seminar meet a specific need in your school or district?

- How relevant was this topic to your professional life?

Process

- How well did the instructional techniques and activities facilitate your understanding of the topic?

- How can you incorporate the activities learned today into your daily professional life?

- Were a variety of learning experiences included in the seminar?

- Was any particular activity memorable? What made it stand out?

Context

- Were the facilities conducive to learning?

- Were the accommodations adequate for the activities involved?

Overall

- Overall, how successful would you consider this seminar? Please include a brief comment or explanation.

- What was the most valuable thing you gained from this seminar experience?

Additional Comments

SOURCE: Adapted from *Evaluating Professional Development* by Thomas R. Guskey, Corwin Press, 2000.

Notes

CORWIN PRESS

The Corwin Press logo—a raven striding across an open book—represents the union of courage and learning. Corwin Press is committed to improving education for all learners by publishing books and other professional development resources for those serving the field of PreK–12 education. By providing practical, hands-on materials, Corwin Press continues to carry out the promise of its motto: **"Helping Educators Do Their Work Better."**